THE HOLY PROPHET'S
KINDNESS TO CHILDREN

By:

Rashid Ahmad Chaudhry

ISLAM INTERNATIONAL PUBLICATIONS LTD

The Holy Prophet's Kindness To Children

Author: Rashid Ahmad Chaudhry

Illustrations: Saba Javed & Ambreen Ahmad

First published in UK in 1989
Reprinted in UK   1990
Present Revised Edition 2004

©Islam International Publications Ltd

Published by:
Islam International Publications Limited
"Islamabad"
Sheephatch Lane
Tilford,Surrey GU102AQ
U.K.

Printed at:
Raqeem Press,
Islamabad, Tilford,Surrey
GU10 2AQ

All rights reserved. No part of this publication may be reproduced, stored in a retrieval system or transmitted in any form or by any means, electronic, mechanical, photo-copying, recording or otherwise, without the prior written permission of the publisher.

ISBN: 1 85372 292 8

CONTENTS

1. Introduction   5
2. Preface to Revised Edition   6
3. Muhammad, peace and blessings of Allah
   be upon him   7
4. Abolishing the custom of killing baby girls   15
5. Respect children   17
6. All children get inheritance   19
7. Education of girls   21
8. Parents to pray for their children   24
9. Care of orphans   27
10. Responsibilities of the guardians   29
11. Do not deprive the legal heirs   31
12. Treat all children fairly   32
13. Be kind to workers: pay their wages promptly   35
14. Affection for children   37
15. Keep your promises   39
16. Consideration towards children   41
17. Punishing children   43
18. Every child is born sinless   45
19. Invoke blessings on the Prophet   47

In The Name Of Allah, Most Gracious, Ever Merciful

INTRODUCTION

The members of the Children's Book Committee have prepared "The Holy Prophet's Kindness To Children". The committee was appointed by Hadhrat Khalifat-ul-Masih IV and worked under his direct supervision and guidance. After his demise the project was continued under the supervision of Hadhrat Mirza Masroor Ahmad, Khalifat-ul-Masih V.

The members of the committee wish to show their gratitude to Hadhrat Mir Muhammad Ismail, a Companion of the Promised Messiah peace be upon him, whose original Urdu book 'Aalam-I-Atfal aur Rahmatul–lil-Aalameen', was published some years back and was acknowledged as one of the best books written for the upbringing of children. The book has indeed inspired us to produce the present work. May Allah shower His blessings on him.

We hope that teachers, parents and children will welcome this book.

The names of the teacher and children have no special significance. They are fictitious.

Muslim readers are urged to say, "May peace and blessings of Allah be upon him" whenever the name of the Holy Prophet Muhammad appears in the text and "peace be upon him" whenever the name of any other Prophet appears in the text.

Book Committee for Children

In the Name of Allah, Most Gracious, Ever Merciful

PREFACE TO REVISED EDITION

Addressing the Holy Prophet of Islam, Muhammad (may peace and blessings of Allah be upon him), Allah says in the Holy Quran, "We have sent thee not but as a mercy for all peoples" (21:108).

The Holy Prophet was indeed an embodiment of Divine mercy. He is a blessing for the whole of mankind, as his message was not confined to a particular era or to a particular people. By leaving priceless teachings as a source of guidance, the Holy Prophet can be regarded as a mercy for his followers, his opponents, for men and women, young and old.

In this revised edition, the members of the Book Committee for Children have taken into consideration some useful suggestions provided by the readers for the improvement of this booklet and have added some interesting incidents from the life of the Holy Prophet of Islam, which showed his extreme kindness to children.

Rashid Ahmad Chaudhry, Chairman of the Book Committee for Children and the members of his team namely Mansoor Saqi, Masroor Ahmad, Salimullah Kahlon, and Maidah Ahmad deserve our thanks for revising the text. May God bless them all.

We hope that this publication will instil in our children the love of the Holy Prophet (may peace and blessings of Allah be upon him).

Munir-ud-Din Shams
Additional Vakil-ut-Tasneef,
London, November 2003

MUHAMMAD

May peace and blessings of Allah be upon him

It was 9`o clock on Friday morning. The bell rang and all the children in the local primary school hurried to their classes. Form 2M had religious studies as their first lesson. As soon as they sat down in their seats their teacher Miss Mitchell entered the room. "We are going to discuss the life of the Prophet of Islam this term," she announced.

She asked the children if they knew where the Holy Prophet was born.
There was no response from the children.
She then asked, "Who can tell me the name of the Founder of Islam?"
Ahmad raised his hand, and said, "The name of the Founder of Islam is Muhammad, may peace and blessings of Allah be upon him".
"Well done," said Miss Mitchell.
She then told the class that the Prophet of Islam was born in a town called Makkah in Saudi Arabia.
Miss Mitchell then asked Angela to point out the country of Arabia on the world map.

Illustration: school

Angela stepped forward and placed her finger on the map.

Miss Mitchell began her story like this:

Muhammad was born at Makkah in Arabia in 570 AD. His grandfather Abdul Muttalib gave him the name Muhammad. He was born an orphan.

"Do you know what an orphan is?" asked Miss Mitchell.

"Miss," said Robin, "A child who has lost his father or mother is called an orphan."

"That is correct" said the teacher.

Muhammad's father Abdullah had died a few months before the birth of the child. Muhammad belonged to a very noble family of Arabia called the Quraish. As was the custom in Arabia in those days, baby Muhammad was handed over by his mother Aamina to a wet nurse called Haleema, to be brought up in the countryside.

"What is a wet nurse?" asked Kim.

"A wet nurse is a woman who is paid to suckle another woman's baby," answered Miss Mitchell.

When Muhammad was six years old his mother died. His grandfather Abdul Muttalib took him into his care, but he too died two years later.

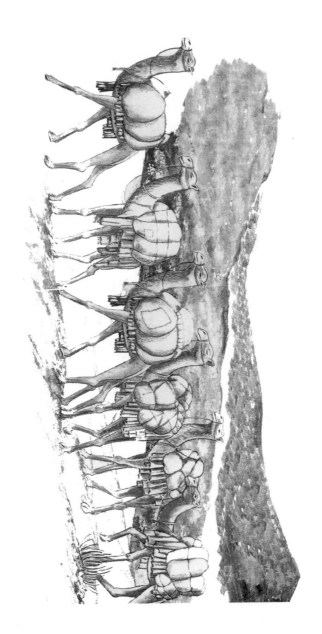

Illustration: Trading caravan

Thereafter his uncle Abu Taalib looked after him. As a boy, Muhammad used to look after the goats and camels in the fields like other Arab youngsters. He was a very noble child. He never told a lie. He was pious, truthful and honest, so much so that he was given the titles AS-SAADIQ meaning "the truthful" and AL-AMEEN, meaning, "the trustworthy", by the people. He tried to help the poor and the weak. He was always respectful to his elders and kind to the young.

Khadijah, a rich widow of Makkah, had heard of the honesty, piety, trustworthiness and high moral character of Muhammad. She decided to employ him as her trade agent. She therefore approached Abu Taalib with the suggestion that he should let his nephew lead a trading caravan of hers to Syria. Abu Taalib consulted Muhammad and they both agreed to the proposal. The business trip was a great success. Muhammad returned with huge profits.

Khadijah was greatly impressed with his honesty and the way he had handled her business affairs. She therefore made him a marriage proposal, which he accepted. At the time of their marriage, Muhammad was twenty-five and Khadijah was forty years old. After the marriage Khadijah gave all her wealth and slaves to Muhammad. Muhammad spent most of the wealth to help the poor and needy and immediately freed all the slaves.

Muslims believe that when Muhammad reached the age of forty, God appointed him as His Messenger. It is said that he often went outside the city of Makkah and spent his time in the worship of God in a cave called Hira. This cave was situated on the top of a mountain about three miles outside Makkah. He was dissatisfied with the way of life which he saw around him in Makkah. It was a corrupt society. The poor and the orphans were totally neglected. People worshipped many gods made of stones or wood. One day when he was praying to God in the cave, the angel Gabriel came and directed him to recite. Muhammad replied that he did not know how to recite. The angel insisted and so Muhammad began to recite as he was instructed. This was the start of the revelation. It was a new experience for Muhammad. This and other revelations, which followed, became parts of the Quran, the Holy Book of the Muslims.

The word "Quran" literally means that which is recited most often. Whenever any portion of the Quran was revealed to Prophet Muhammad he learnt it by heart. Many of his followers did the same. Some of them even wrote the verses on anything available like pieces of leather, bark of trees or stones.

"What is REVELATION?" asked Susan.

Miss Mitchell explained, "Revelation is the Divine Knowledge that is conveyed verbally to man by God. The Prophet of Islam could neither read nor write, but God gave him a great amount of knowledge through revelation."

She continued: Very few people accepted him in the beginning. Most of the people of Makkah rejected him and ridiculed him. He lived in Makkah for thirteen years. During this time he and his followers were persecuted. When the persecution became very intense, God commanded him to leave Makkah. He therefore went to Madinah, a city where Islam had already spread. This event is known as Hijra in Islamic history. The Islamic calendar starts from the date the Prophet of Islam migrated from Makkah to Madinah. When the people of Makkah saw that Islam was flourishing in Madinah, they attacked Madinah a number of times in order to destroy the Muslims. Against all odds, the Muslims won all battles. Finally the Muslim forces, under the command of the Prophet of Islam, entered Makkah victorious.

The Prophet died at the age of sixty-three in 633 AD. By that time Islam had spread throughout Arabia. The Prophet of Islam showed kindness to everyone, even to his enemies, but he was extremely kind to children.

The pupils were so absorbed in the story that they did not even hear the bell, which had already gone, marking the end of the lesson. The teacher then said, "Next week, those children who want to take part should relate one incident from the life of the Prophet of Islam, which shows his kindness and love for children."

1

ABOLISHING THE CUSTOM OF KILLING BABY GIRLS

Next Friday when the class assembled, Ayesha stood up and said, "One of the great favours bestowed by our Holy Prophet on mankind was that he abolished the custom of killing baby girls. I come from Arabia. In the old days, before the time of the Holy Prophet of Islam, there lived certain tribes in Arabia, which considered the birth of girls as a disgrace to their families, so some of the chiefs used to kill the girls soon after their birth. They thought that they would save their honour by such an action. The Holy Prophet abolished this cruel custom. He has, thus, shown great kindness to children, especially girls. May peace and blessings of Allah be upon the Holy Prophet of Islam."

As soon as Ayesha finished her story, Satnam raised his hand and said, "Miss, my mother told me that in India too, there were some people that used to kill the baby girls. Even now-a-days, on the birth of a girl, people are not as happy as on the birth of a boy."

Miss Mitchell said, "Yes Satnam, you are right. We are therefore very grateful to the Prophet of Islam for abolishing this cruel custom."

2

RESPECT YOUR CHILDREN

It was Ahmad's turn next. He related a Saying of the Holy Prophet of Islam, in which he had instructed his followers to respect their children.

The Holy Prophet is reported to have said, "Respect your children and cultivate in them the best of manners."

Ahmad said, "It is a pity that most parents disregard this golden principle. They sometimes ignore their children completely. There are parents who love their children very much, feed them well, give them decent clothes to wear and generally look after them properly but do not care for their feelings.

The Holy Prophet has instructed that parents should not hurt the feelings of their children. They should be kind to them. Moreover they should openly discuss with them those matters, which are important to them. This would surely develop in them the feelings of dignity, self-respect and high moral qualities. The Holy Prophet has emphasized to parents that they should educate their children in the best possible manner and develop in them the respect for elders. This is a great favour of the Holy Prophet on children. May peace and blessings of Allah be upon him."

Miss Mitchell thanked Ahmad for bringing these important teachings of the noble Prophet of Islam to the notice of the class.

3

EVERY CHILD GETS INHERITANCE

Imran was eager to speak next. He said, "The Holy Prophet taught his followers that when a person dies, his property should be distributed fairly among all his children and the younger ones should not be left out."

It was a custom in Arabia in those days that the elder son inherited everything, making the younger ones dependant on him. Even today in some countries it is the eldest son only, who inherits the wealth his parents leave behind.

Imran said, "We should be extremely grateful to the Holy Prophet who has instructed Muslims not to differentiate between children. In a Muslim Society therefore, all children get the share of their parental wealth and property. I am the youngest of my brothers, yet I am entitled to an equal share of my father's estate. We should therefore praise the wisdom of the Holy Prophet for such beautiful teachings. May peace and blessings of Allah be upon him."

Tahira raised her hand and said, "I would like to add a bit more to what has been said already. Islam is the only religion, which has given a detailed system of inheritance. It defines the people who inherit and the share each person receives in a particular situation. Moreover Islam is the first religion, to give women the right of inheritance. It makes daughters, along with sons, heirs to the property left by their parents."

Tahira continued, "Because of these teachings, not only girls, but also women in general, were given proper inheritance rights."

Miss Mitchell said, "It seems that the Prophet of Islam was very keen on improving the condition of women in society and on securing for them a position of dignity and fair and equal treatment."

4

EDUCATION OF GIRLS

The next pupil Maryam stood up and said, "I would like to say something about the education of girls. The Prophet of Islam has laid great stress on the education of girls. He instructed Muslims to make sure that they received a good education. In this way, not only would they become good mothers and bring up their children in the best possible manner, but also being educated, they would be able to contribute more to society."

She said, "Acting upon this Saying of the Holy Prophet Muhammad, my mother's father made sure that my mother received a good education both academic as well as religious. As a result, she excels most of her male colleagues in her work. We should be grateful to Prophet Muhammad who instructed Muslims to educate their daughters. May peace and blessings of Allah be upon him."

John raised his hand and said, "Miss! Does it mean that the Prophet of Islam was not in favour of boys' education?"

Illustration
Girls should receive a good education.

Miss Mitchell said, "No, that is not the case. The Prophet of Islam lived in a society where women were looked down upon. They had no status in the society. The Prophet of Islam, therefore, emphasized the education of girls."

Lailah raised her hand and said, "Miss! I come from Afghanistan. There was a time when the government did not allow girls' education in schools. The girls' schools were closed. The instruction of the Holy Prophet that "Acquisition of knowledge is obligatory upon every Muslim male and female" was completely ignored.

Miss Mitchell said, "I know that seeking of knowledge is considered to be a religious obligation in Islam. This is a very important topic indeed. If someone else wants to contribute something please do so."

Zoya said, "My Sunday School teacher has told us a Saying of the Holy Prophet of Islam. He is reported to have said, "No gift, among all the gifts of a father to his child, is better than education."

Miss Mitchell said, "Thank you Zoya for this information."

5

PARENTS TO PRAY FOR THEIR CHILDREN

Ambreen then reminded the class of a Saying of the Holy Prophet, in which he instructed Muslim parents to pray for their children. She said that the Holy Prophet had mentioned special prayers for that purpose. Some prayers are:

"O Allah keep me and my progeny away from worshipping idols" (14:36)

"Lord make me and everyone of my progeny steadfast in observing Prayer." (14:41)

"Our Lord grant us of our spouses and children, the delight of our eyes and make each of us a leader of the righteous" (25:75).

Ambreen said "May peace and blessings of Allah be upon the Holy Prophet who taught these wonderful prayers to Muslims."

Ayesha said, "Let me remind you of another Saying of the Holy Prophet. He is reported to have said, "Three prayers are accepted by God without any doubt. The prayer of a father for his children, the prayer of a person on a journey and the prayer of a person who is persecuted."

Miss Mitchell thanked Ambreen and Ayesha.

Barbara inquired," What is meant by progeny?"

The teacher explained, "Progeny means the descendants of a person. 'My progeny' means my children and the children of my children and so on. The Prophet of Islam has instructed his followers to pray not only for themselves but also for their coming generations."

6

CARE OF ORPHANS

Waleed then got up and said, "I am an orphan. My parents died a long time ago. My foster parents looked after me. They were always very kind to me. They brought me up like their own child. I am very grateful to Allah and his Messenger Muhammad, the Holy Prophet of Islam, for the concern shown about the care of orphans. Allah says in the Holy Quran, 'They ask you about the orphans. Tell them: The promotion of their welfare is an act of great goodness. There is no harm in your living together with them, for they are your brethren, and Allah will know him who seeks to promote their welfare and also him who seeks to do them harm,' (2:221)

The Prophet of Islam said, "I and the one who looks after the needs of an orphan and brings him or her up in the best possible manner, will be together in heaven like two fingers of a hand.' And the narrator raised his forefinger and middle finger by way of illustration."

Waleed explained that the Holy Prophet had given detailed instructions to Muslims as to how orphans should be treated. Waleed said "The Holy Prophet himself was an orphan; therefore he understood their feelings. May peace and blessings of Allah be upon him."

Tariq said, "I have a book which contains the Sayings of the Holy Prophet. In one of them he is reported to have said: The best Muslim home is that in which an orphan is treated with kindness, and the worst is that in which an orphan is treated unkindly."

Miss Mitchell said, "The bringing up of orphans is a very delicate and important matter. Islam lays great emphasis on the care of orphans. It tells us that they should be treated as members of the family and be brought up in the best possible manner. It is the responsibility of those who take up the role of a guardian to provide for the orphans in their care a good education and take good care of their property until they are old enough to manage their own property."

7

RESPONSIBILITIES OF THE GUARDIANS

It was Abdullah's turn next. He related the following Saying of the Holy Prophet:

"O ye People, everyone of you is a guardian and is responsible to God Almighty for the people in his care."

Miss Mitchell said, "Abdullah can you explain what it means?"

Abdullah said, "It means that those in authority are answerable to God Almighty for the treatment of the people in their care. Every person has some authority over others but he also has some duties and responsibilities towards those who are in his care. For example the Imam, or the religious leader, who is to look after the people will be asked about his people and the husband, who is to look after the members of his family, will be asked about the people of his family. The wife, who is to look after the household and children, will be asked about the household and the children. Similarly the servant or the employee will be answerable about all that was given in his charge.

All such people like teachers, parents, brothers, sisters, employers, and elders should discharge their duties in the best possible manner. Those who look after children should make sure that the children acquire good habits and receive a good education. We as children should be extremely grateful to the Holy Prophet of Islam for such beautiful teachings. May peace and blessings of Allah be upon him."

8

DO NOT DEPRIVE THE LEGAL HEIRS

The next person to speak was Khalid. He stood up and said, "My uncle is a rich man and owns a large property. He has no children of his own. My aunt adopted a child from her close relations and tried to make him the sole heir. This would have deprived us and all the other legal heirs from the share in the property of my uncle. When my uncle consulted the Imam, he told him that Islam does not recognise the inheritance rights of an adopted son. My aunt therefore changed her mind. We were therefore not deprived of our share. We thank Allah and His Prophet for this justice. May peace and blessings of Allah be upon him."

Tony, who was sitting next to Khalid, said, "Miss, who is an Imam?"

Miss Mitchell replied, "The Imam is a person who leads Muslims in Prayer. He is a religious leader, to whom Muslims go for advice in religious matters."

9

TREAT ALL CHILDREN FAIRLY

Sameen spoke next. She informed the class that the Holy Prophet of Islam has told Muslims to be fair in their dealings with all children. She related an incident from the life of the Holy Prophet. She said "Once a Companion by the name of Bashir approached the Holy Prophet along with his son Nu'maan and said, 'Will you please be my witness that I have given one of my servants as a gift to this son of mine'.
The Holy Prophet inquired, 'What about your other sons? Have you given a similar gift to each one of them?' Bashir replied, 'No.' The Holy Prophet then remarked, 'I cannot be a witness to such an unjust act.'
From this incident we see that the Holy Prophet was very keen to see that parents treat all their children fairly and equally. May peace and blessings of Allah be upon him. "
Satnam said, "Miss, my sister does not like the toys which I like, so my father

brings different toys for her. Is that alright?"

"Yes," said Miss Mitchell, as long as both of you get toys of your choice, it is okay but supposing one of you doesn't get anything at all, that is unfair."

Paper boy

10

BE KIND TO SERVANTS.
PAY THEIR WAGES PROMPTLY

It was Mansoor's turn next. He began his story like this:

"My brother delivers newspapers in the morning before school. If he makes a mistake, he is told off, shouted at, and sometimes fined by the newsagent. He is not always paid on time. The shopkeeper withholds his wages sometimes for weeks. The other day when I went to the mosque, I heard the Imam saying that during the days of the Holy Prophet, there lived a boy called Anas. He was one of the most devoted followers of the Holy Prophet. His mother had left him in the company of the Holy Prophet, when he was ten years old. He had the good fortune of serving in his household for many years. He related that the Holy Prophet had never told him off for not doing something, which he ought to have done or for doing something he should not have done.

Anas also claimed that he never saw anyone else who would show such kindness to children."

Mansoor said, "This incident shows that the Holy Prophet was extraordinarily kind towards children. May peace and blessings of Allah be upon him."

Sarah raised her hand and said, "The Holy Prophet had laid great emphasis on the rights of the workers. He is reported to have said, 'Pay wages to the worker before his sweat is dry.' A shopkeeper, therefore, has no right to withhold the wages of the boy who delivers newspapers for him."

Miss Mitchell added, "The teachings of Islam are beautiful in this regard. Employers should make prompt payment of the wages of their workers."

11

AFFECTION FOR CHILDREN

Humairah related an incident from the life of the Holy Prophet. "Once the Holy Prophet's grandsons came to see him. He picked them up and kissed them and cuddled them affectionately. A Bedouin who was watching him said: 'O Messenger of Allah, we have never shown affection to our children like you have shown.' The Prophet replied, 'If you are deprived of love and mercy for your children, what can I do?' "

Humairah continued, "This incident also shows us that the Holy Prophet was very kind and affectionate towards children. May peace and blessings of Allah be upon him."

Winston asked, "Miss what is a Bedouin?"

The teacher replied, "Bedouin are Arabs who live in the deserts and move from one place to another like gypsies. They have no permanent place to live."

Ahmad said, "If we look at the life of the Holy Prophet we will find that he was very kind to everyone. Children too, loved his company. Seeing him in the street the children would come close to him jumping with joy. He would pick them up one by one, cuddle them, kiss them and pray for them. It is related that very often when he was riding a horse or a camel, he would carry his grandson on the horse either at his back or in his front or sometimes on his shoulders.

Very often the Companions of the Holy Prophet would see Hasan, his grandson, seated on his right thigh while Usama, the son of his freed slave Zaid, seated on his left thigh. He would embrace both of them lovingly and supplicate, 'O Lord! Shower Thy Mercy and Grace on both of them.'

Sometimes it so happened that a mother handed him over her baby to seek his blessing. While he was holding a baby in his arms, the baby wetted. The Holy Prophet did not mind, but he immediately got his clothes washed.

In fact the love and kindness that the world has witnessed at his hand was matchless. No other person equals to him in this regard. May peace and blessings of Allah be upon him."

12

KEEP YOUR PROMISES

Naseer began his story like this. "Once the Holy Prophet went to the house of one of his Companions. The woman of the house called her son, who was playing outside, in order to present him before the Holy Prophet to seek his blessings. She said, 'Come here, I will give you something to eat.' The Holy Prophet inquired, 'what are you promising to give him?'

She replied, 'A dried date.' The Holy Prophet remarked, 'If you promise something to a child and you do not keep your promise, you commit the same sin as the one who tells a lie.' "

Naseer continued, "This Saying of the Holy Prophet tells us that we should always keep our promises. May peace and blessings of Allah be upon him."

Mary said, "Every religion tells us that we should keep our promises and speak the truth. Telling a lie is regarded as a great sin."

The teacher explained, "To tell a lie is not a good thing, and once the habit is developed, it is very difficult to get rid of. Generally, children acquire this habit by copying their elders. So grown ups should set a good example in front of children and refrain from telling lies."

Sarah asked permission to speak and related a Saying in which the Holy Prophet said, "Truth guides to virtue and virtue guides to paradise. A person persists in telling the truth till in the sight of God he is named Truthful. Telling lies leads to vice and vice leads to the Fire. A person goes on telling lies till in the sight of God he is named a Liar."

13

CONSIDERATION TOWARDS CHILDREN

Zoya related an incident from the life of the Holy Prophet. She said, "Once the Holy Prophet remarked that he wanted to prolong supplications, when he was leading the Prayer but he cut it short, when he heard a child crying. He did not want the child and the child's mother to suffer. This shows how sensitive and considerate the Holy Prophet was towards children. May peace and blessings of Allah be upon him."

Aamina raised her hand and said, "The Holy Prophet has told us that we should be respectful to our elders and kind to the young. He is reported to have said, 'One who has no compassion for our young ones and does not recognize the rights of our elders is not of us.' "

Sarah said, "Miss! I know a Saying of the Holy Prophet. Ayesha, the wife of the Holy Prophet related: A poor woman came to me with her two daughters. I had nothing in the house to give to her except dates.

So I gave her three dates. She gave one to each girl and raised the third to her own mouth to eat. The girls asked her for it, so she broke it into two parts and gave half to one and the other half to the other. I was astonished at her sacrifice and mentioned this incident to the Holy Prophet. The Holy Prophet said: God will bestow paradise upon that woman on account of the consideration she had shown towards her daughters."

14

PUNISHING CHILDREN

The next person to speak was Tariq. He told the class that the Holy Prophet forbade anyone to hit a child on the face. He said, "I was watching a TV programme the other day. There were many cases reported, where parents were so annoyed with the behaviour of their children that they lost their temper and hit them on their faces. In some countries, even today elders hit children as a punishment, for any wrong they have done. Sometimes this leaves a scar on their faces or causes other serious injuries. The Holy Prophet of Islam, who stood for the cause of children, forbade anyone to hit them on their faces. This shows the kindness and love of the Holy Prophet for children. May peace and blessings of Allah be upon the Holy Prophet who gave us such beautiful teachings."

Miss Mitchell said, "We all know that the face is a sensitive part of our body, and hitting on the face can cause serious harm. We should therefore never hit children on their faces."

15

EVERY CHILD IS BORN SINLESS

Zain was to speak next. He got up from his seat and said, "In Islam we believe that all children are born sinless."

John said "Miss! What do Christians believe?"

Miss Mitchell explained, "The majority of Christians believe in the hereditary sin theory. They say that Adam and Eve sinned. As a result their progeny began to inherit sin and ever since all children of Adam are born sinners."

Zain said, "According to Islamic teachings, each person is responsible for his or her actions and is accountable to God. The Holy Quran says that no one can bear the burden of another. (35:19)

If a man commits a sin, punishment of that sin should be given to him alone and to no one else. This is the fundamental principle of justice. According to Islam, therefore, every child is born sinless, as the sin of one person cannot be passed on to any one else. It is his environment, the ideas and beliefs of his parents and the training he receives from them subsequently that make him good or bad."

Hamzah was sitting next to him. He added, "The Holy Prophet of Islam is reported to have said, 'Every child is born in harmony with nature. It is his parents who turn him into a Jew, a fire-worshipper or a Christian.' "

He said that we should be grateful to the Holy Prophet of Islam as he had removed the stigma of sin from every new-born and declared that every child that comes into this world is sinless and innocent.

16

INVOKE BLESSINGS ON THE PROPHET

Akbar was last to speak. He said, "We have covered one aspect of the life of the Holy Prophet. We have seen that he was very affectionate towards children. We have listened to his various Sayings, and teachings, which tell us how children should be brought up. Islam is a complete code of life. It mentions the rights and duties of the rulers as well as of their subjects, the rights and duties of husbands and wives, of traders and their customers.

We, as children, have much to learn from Islam if we want to make our lives successful. We have to act upon the teachings brought by the Holy Prophet of Islam if we want to create a healthy and happy society.

God has sent the Holy Prophet as a 'mercy for mankind.'

He was a blessing not only for his followers but also for his opponents. He was a mercy for animals and even for plants. It is our duty therefore to pay tribute to such a person and offer salutation of peace to him."

Akbar said that the Holy Quran states, 'Allah sends down His blessings on the Prophet, and His angels constantly invoke Allah's blessings on him. Do you, O believers, also invoke Allah's blessings on him and offer him the salutation of peace.' (33:57)

"In obedience to this Divine command, Muslims all over the world pray for him and invoke the blessings of God on him. They say: Shower Thy blessings, O Allah, on Muhammad and his people as Thou have showered Thy blessings on Abraham and the people of Abraham.

Prosper O Allah, Muhammad and his people as Thy have prospered Abraham and the people of Abraham. You are indeed Praiseworthy, the Gracious."

Sita, Billy, Susan and Metori all were eager to tell their stories, but the teacher looked at her watch and said, "There seems to be no time left for further discussion today. We will therefore postpone the discussion till next time."

The bell rang and the teacher dismissed the class.